Flowers

by Grace Hansen

abdopublishing.com

Published by Abdo Kids, a division of ABDO, PO Box 398166, Minneapolis, Minnesota 55439.

Copyright © 2016 by Abdo Consulting Group, Inc. International copyrights reserved in all countries. No part of this book may be reproduced in any form without written permission from the publisher.

Printed in the United States of America, North Mankato, Minnesota.

102015

012016

Photo Credits: iStock, Shutterstock

Production Contributors: Teddy Borth, Jennie Forsberg, Grace Hansen

Design Contributors: Laura Mitchell, Dorothy Toth

Library of Congress Control Number: 2015942103

Cataloging-in-Publication Data

Hansen, Grace.

 Flowers / Grace Hansen.

  p. cm. -- (Plant anatomy)

ISBN 978-1-68080-135-4 (lib. bdg.)

Includes index.

1. Flowers--Juvenile literature.   I. Title.

575.6--dc23

2015942103

Table of Contents

Flowers Make Flowers

A flower is a part of some plants. A flower has a big job to do. It is to make more flowers.

5

Flowers **pollinate** to make more flowers. The movement of pollen starts this process.

7

Pollen moves in many ways.
People and wind move pollen.
Water moves pollen. Insects
move pollen, too.

9

Pollinators

Some flowers are colorful.

They can also smell good.

These things attract insects.

A bee lands on a flower.

Pollen sticks to its body.

Then it flies to another flower.

13

The pollen moves with the bee.
Flowers have **stigma**. They are
sticky. They grab onto the pollen.

anther

stigma

15

Pollen moves through the **style** to the **ovary**. This is where **fertilization** happens.

16

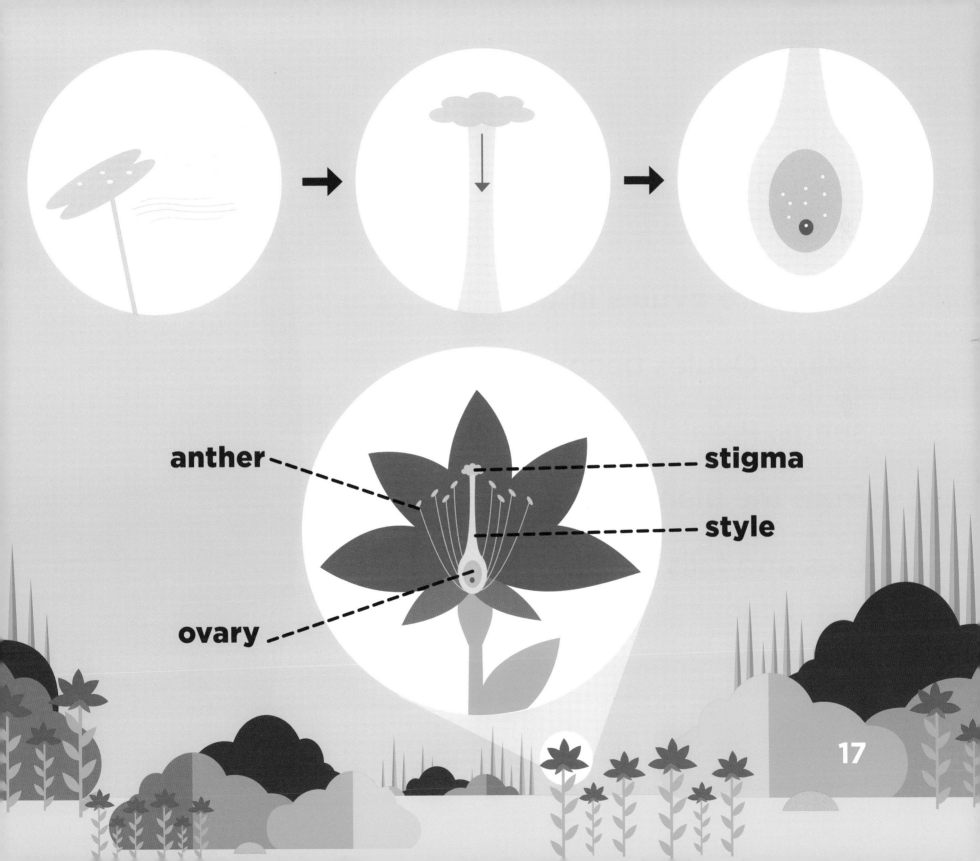

anther

stigma

style

ovary

17

There are **ovules** in the **ovary**. Ovules become seeds. Petals fall away from the plant. The plant dies and falls to the ground.

New Plants!

The seeds spread out on the ground. Some are moved to far places. The seeds grow to become new plants!

Flower Reproduction

1

anther

2

stigma

pollen moves from an
anther to a stigma

3

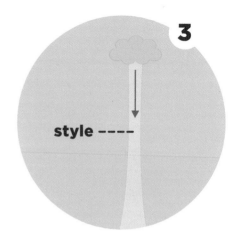

style - - - -

pollen moves
down the style

4

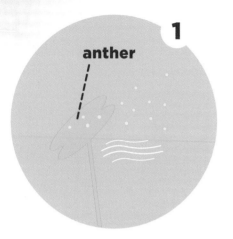

ovary

ovule

pollen enters the ovary
and fertilizes an ovule

5

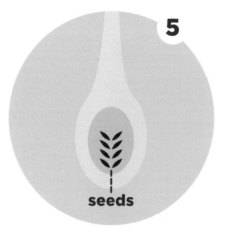

seeds

fertilized ovules
become seeds

6

flower

seeds spread out and
become new flowers

Glossary

anther – the part of the stamen of a flower that holds pollen.

fertilization – when pollen enters an ovule.

ovary – the large and round bottom part of the pistil that holds the ovules.

ovule – the part of the ovary that after fertilization becomes a seed.

pollinate – to give a plant pollen from another plant of the same kind so that seeds can be made.

stigma – part of the pistil of a flower which receives pollen grains.

style – part of the pistil of a flower that holds up the stigma.

Index

abdokids.com

Use this code to log on to abdokids.com and access crafts, games, videos, and more!

Abdo Kids Code:
PFK1354